Bessie Coleman
Trailblazing Pilot

by Carol Alexander

Content Consultant
Nanci R. Vargus, Ed.D.
Professor Emeritus, University of Indianapolis

Reading Consultant
Jeanne M. Clidas, Ph.D.
Reading Specialist

Children's Press®
An Imprint of Scholastic Inc.

Library of Congress Cataloging-in-Publication Data
Alexander, Carol, 1955-
Bessie Coleman/by Carol Alexander; poem by Jodie Shepherd.
    pages cm — (Rookie biographies)
Includes index.
ISBN 978-0-531-22545-5 (library binding) — ISBN 978-0-531-22634-6 (pbk.)
    1. Coleman, Bessie, 1896-1926—Juvenile literature. 2. African American women air pilots—Biography—Juvenile literature. 3. Air pilots—United States—Biography—Juvenile literature. I. Shepherd, Jodie. II. Title.
TL540.C546A44 2016
    629.13092—dc23 [B]   2015020966

Produced by Spooky Cheetah Press
Poem by Jodie Shepherd
Design by Keith Plechaty

Printed in China 62

SCHOLASTIC, CHILDREN'S PRESS, ROOKIE BIOGRAPHIES®, and associated logos are trademarks and/or registered trademarks of Scholastic Inc.

1 2 3 4 5 6 7 8 9 10 R 25 24 23 22 21 20 19 18 17 16

Photographs ©: cover: Michael Ochs Archives/Getty Images; 3 top left: catwalker/Shutterstock, Inc.; 3 top right: Kletr/Shutterstock, Inc.; 3 bottom: Los Angeles Public Library; 4: Smithsonian National Air and Space Museum (NASM 92-13721); 8: The Granger Collection; 11: Corbis Images; 12: The Abbott Sengstacke Family Papers/Getty Images; 15: ullstein bild/The Image Works; 16: Marka/Superstock, Inc.; 19, 20: Underwood & Underwood/Corbis Images; 23: Smithsonian National Air and Space Museum (NASM 99-15415); 24: Smithsonian National Air and Space Museum (NASM 79-12283); 27: Smithsonian National Air and Space Museum (NASM 9A00624); 28: Smithsonian National Air and Space Museum (NASM SI 88-7993); 29, 30 top left: Underwood & Underwood/Corbis Images; 30 top right: Smithsonian National Air and Space Museum (NASM 99-15415); 31 top: Smithsonian National Air and Space Museum (NASM 92-13721); 31 center top: Minnesota Historical Society/Corbis Images; 31 center bottom: John Vachon/Library of Congress; 31 bottom: Alfred Eisenstaedt/Getty Images.

Map by Terra Carta

Table of Contents

Meet Bessie Coleman

When Bessie Coleman was young, no one encouraged her to follow her dreams. At the time, African-American children were not expected to succeed.

But Bessie would not let anyone hold her back. She became the first-ever black female pilot in the world. In fact, she became a world-famous **aviator**.

Bessie was born in Atlanta, Texas, on January 26, 1892. She was one of 13 children. When she was two years old, Bessie's family moved west to Waxahachie.

Bessie's grandparents had been slaves. Her parents were **sharecroppers**. They grew cotton crops for other farmers.

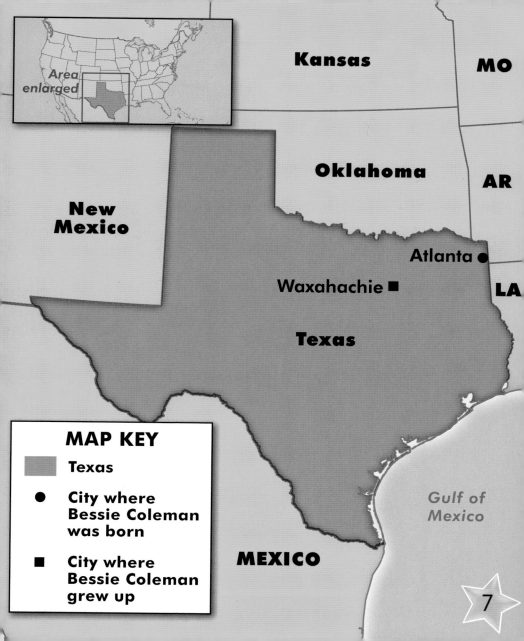

Kansas

MO

Oklahoma

AR

New
Mexico

Atlanta ●

Waxahachie ■

LA

Texas

Gulf of
Mexico

MEXICO

MAP KEY

Texas

● City where
Bessie Coleman
was born

■ City where
Bessie Coleman
grew up

Area
enlarged

a school for black children

FAST FACT!

School closed when it was time to pick the cotton. Bessie and the other children had to work in the fields.

Times were hard for people like the Colemans. **Segregation** was practiced in the South. That meant black people and white people were kept apart. Black people were often very poor.

Bessie went to school in a one-room schoolhouse. It was just for black children. She had to walk four miles (6.4 kilometers) each way to get there and home.

A New Start

After school, Coleman went to work. She saved enough money to start college in 1910. But soon she ran out of money. She had to leave school. Two of her brothers lived in Chicago. She moved in with them. She got a job as a manicurist. But she was not very happy. All the time, Coleman dreamed of something bigger.

Chicago was a busy city when Coleman moved there. It was home to many African Americans.

MAJESTIC
THEATRE

SUPREME
VAUDEVILLE

KARYL NORMAN
EMMA CARUS
HEDEGUS SISTERS
CHAS. OLCOTT & CO

11

Soon Coleman's luck began to change. She became friends with Robert Abbott. He published the most important African-American newspaper in the United States. It was called the *Chicago Defender*. Coleman's friendship with Abbott would change her life. He helped her follow her dream to become a pilot.

This is a photo of Coleman's friend Robert Abbott.

A Dream of Flight

While Coleman was living in Chicago, the United States entered World War I. This was the first time in history planes were used to fight in a war. The war ended in 1918. American pilots were returning home. They bragged about their daring flights. Coleman dreamed of taking to the sky herself. But no one in America would teach a young black woman how to fly.

fighter pilots
in World War I

In 1920, Coleman traveled to France. She was accepted to the country's top flight school. Coleman knew the training would take all of her savings. And she was the only black student in her class. Still, she was determined to succeed.

Frenchwoman Raymonde de Laroche (1882–1919) was the first woman pilot in the world.

Taking Off!

Coleman knew that learning to fly was dangerous. She had to practice on a plane that was old and shaky. One day, Coleman saw another student crash. The accident left her shaken, but she did not stop training.

On June 15, 1921, Coleman received her international pilot's license. She flew in air shows all over Europe.

Coleman became famous. Her many fans nicknamed her "Brave Bess" and "Queen Bess."

Coleman returned to the U.S. in 1921. With her pilot's license, she was confident she could find work. She was wrong. Few people were willing to hire a black female pilot.

The next year, Coleman returned to Europe for more training. She practiced doing stunts and aerial tricks. This type of flying was called **barnstorming**. Coleman was a well-known aviator by the time she returned home again.

Brave Bess

Coleman had proven herself. Now it was easier to find work in America. Her first air show was on Labor Day, 1922.

The following year, Coleman was seriously hurt in a plane crash. But three months later, she was ready to fly again.

This photo shows Coleman with one of her supporters.

Coleman had an exciting year in 1925. She flew in a lot of air shows. She amazed her many fans. Coleman also gave talks about flying. She performed all over the country. But she would not appear in places where there was segregation.

Coleman was famous now. She wanted to help people of color. She planned to open a flight school for African Americans.

Coleman's story ended much too soon. On April 30, 1926, she and another pilot, William D. Wills, flew to Orlando, Florida. Wills was at the controls while Coleman sat in the cockpit. She was looking for places to perform her next air show. Wills lost control of the plane. Both he and Coleman were killed.

At Coleman's funeral, 10,000 people came to pay their respects to the daring pilot.

In 1929, William J. Powell (right) founded the Bessie Coleman Aero Club.

Timeline of Bessie Coleman's Life

1920
attends flight training school in France

1892
born on January 26

1921
receives international pilot's license

In 1977, the Bessie Coleman Aviators Club was founded. Every year, black pilots honor Coleman by flying over her grave.

Bessie Coleman is remembered as a woman who succeeded against great odds. She is a role model who believed in a bright future for African Americans.

1923
seriously injured in a plane crash

1926
dies on April 30

A Poem About Bessie Coleman

Bessie had a dream of flying.

Some said there was no use trying.

Did she listen? She could not care less.

This daring aviator became "Brave Bess."

You Can Follow Your Dreams

- Work hard to meet your goals. Do not be discouraged if it takes a while for you to be successful.

- Be confident. If you believe in yourself, you can accomplish great things!

Glossary

aviator (AY-vee-ay-tuhr): someone who flies an aircraft

barnstorming (BARN-storm-ing): traveling from place to place to perform in exhibitions and showcase flying stunts

segregation (seh-grih-GAY-shun): separation of people of different races within a society

sharecroppers (SHAYR-krah-pers): farmers who raise crops for the people who own the land

Index

Facts for Now

Visit this Scholastic Web site for more information on Bessie Coleman:
www.factsfornow.scholastic.com
Enter the keywords **Bessie Coleman**

About the Author

Carol Alexander has written both fiction and nonfiction for children and young adults. Her poetry appears in many magazines and books. She has taught in colleges around the New York City area and now works in publishing. She lives in New York with her family and pets.